Read, Write and Spell Book 4

Medium Frequency Words
by Heather Bell

Introduction

Read Write and Spell Medium Frequency Words Book 4 is one of a series of six books designed to reinforce the high and medium frequency words as identified by The National Literacy Strategy. Books 1 to 5 contain photocopiable worksheets designed as an aid for the busy primary classroom teacher, preparing word level work for the twenty minute independent session of the literacy hour. Activities include word crosses, word searches, proof reading, open ended word investigations, sentence construction, use of joined handwriting and Look, Say, Cover, Write, Check, spelling strategies. The words covered in this book can be found on the back cover and/or in the Pupil/Class record on page 3.

Topical Resources publishes a range of Educational Materials for use in Primary Schools and Pre-School Nurseries and Playgroups.

For latest catalogue:
Tel: 01772 863158 or
Fax: 01772 866153

Copyright © 1998 Heather Bell
Illustrated by John Hutchinson.

Printed in Great Britain for "Topical Resources", Publishers of Educational Materials, P.O. Box 329, Broughton, Preston, PR3 5LT by T.Snape & Company Ltd, Boltons Court, Preston, England. Typeset by Artworks, 69 Worden Lane, Leyland, Lancashire. PR5 2BD Tel: 01772 431010

First Published September 1998
ISBN 1 872977 37 5

Jean H

Contents

Teacher's Notes Book 4

The purpose of this book is to reinforce the medium frequency words as listed in "The National Literacy Strategy". The photocopiable worksheets are designed as an aid for the busy primary classroom teacher, preparing word level work for the twenty minute independent session of the literacy hour. By using the activities in this book, the children will encounter each word at least four times - within the activity sheets, "Look, Say, Cover, Write, Check" word strips, and proof reading passages. It should be emphasised that the words need to be taught in a variety of ways, if the children are to retain them.

Cursive Handwriting

Although the words on the worksheets are printed, the children should be encouraged to complete the worksheets in the cursive handwriting style of the school. This is of great importance, as research shows that the teaching of spelling should be linked to handwriting, as fully cursive script aids recall of letter order. Again, the "Look, Say ,Cover, Write, Check" word strips are printed. However, it would be useful for the class teacher to write each word cursively below, or in place of, the printed version, in the school's adopted style, before photocopying. The child will copy the cursive version rather than the printed one.

Reinforcing the Medium Frequency Words

Personal Targets

At the front of the book there is a "My Target Words Sheet." Each child could be given a number of the medium frequency words as a personal goal to achieve in a set number of weeks. It is important to consider carefully whether the words given are achievable in the time allowed. The child with special educational needs may only be given five or six words whereas the child with a good visual memory could be given twenty or more. These personal target words could be added into weekly spelling lists or could be sent home as part of the homework programme.

Word Games

Simple word games could be devised as a fun way to aid the learning of the words e.g. snap, pairs, word bingo etc.

Mnemonics

A mnemonic is a device to aid memory, for instance to learn particular spelling patterns or spellings. These are a useful tool in helping the child remember the more difficult medium frequency words .
Alphabet mnemonics - like **O U L**ucky **D**uck, for remembering the spelling of w**ould**, c**ould** and sh**ould**
.
Exaggerated pronounciation of words - like Wednes-day.

Visual mnemonics - like ju^mp

More Useful Mnemonics e.g.

because- **b**ig **e**lephants **c**an **a**lways **u**nderstand sma elephants
people - **p**eople **e**at **o**blong **p**izzas **l**ooking **e**ast
would, could ,should - **O U** **L**ittle **D**arling
Tuesday - **U E**at **S**weets Day
Thursday - **U R S**illy Day
found - **O U N**aughty **D**og I've found you
young- **YOU** are young
eight - **E**veryone **I**s **G**oing **H**ome **T**onight
great - it is gr**EAT** to eat
hear/here - you h**EAR** with your ears

Useful Word Cards - Another means of reinforcing the medium frequency words is to have them printed on cards These can be kept either by individuals or in the "tidy baskets" on group tables so that the children have access to them at all times, whether writing a story or producing a piece of History, Geography or Science work.

Use of Personal Dictionaries - It is useful for the children to make a bank of words which have given them problems These can be added into their Personal Dictionaries.

Classroom Word Bank -After marking pupils' work the teacher will be aware of common class spelling mistakes. A few of these can be highlighted and displayed on a "Word Bank" noticeboard in the classroom.

The Pupil / Class Record Sheet

This is designed to help the class teacher keep a record of children's achievements and to aid in the planning of future work. It would be useful at the beginning of the year to test the children to see which of the words they are already able to spell and thus aid planning of future work. When a child has been tested three times on new words and spelt them correctly, the word could be recorded as learned. This sort of record is an invaluable resource for the setting of special needs Individual Education Plans.

Look, Say, Cover, Write, Check Spelling Strategy

This book contains a number of pages introducing the Look, Say, Cover, Write, Check Spelling Strategy. Teachers may enlarge, extend or change the words on these sheets to make these sheets appropriate to the needs of their class. Again, the class teacher should emphasise the importance of cursive script when practising a word.

Proof Reading

Proof reading is an excellent strategy for making pupils aware of the importance of correct spelling and punctuation. It is most effective if pupils are given the opportunity to work on the passage individually and then compare their work with a partner. After two pupils have studied the same passage together, an element of competition can be introduced by seeing who has found the most mistakes when comparing results with another pair of pupils. This activity can be extended to even larger groups or it can become a whole class activity.

Pupil/Class Record

Name _____

Date begun _____

We can assume a word has been learned when it has been either **tested** or **used correctly** at least three times.

	Tick or Date				Tick or Date				Tick or Date		
above				goes				stopped			
across				gone				such			
almost				half				suddenly			
along				heard				think			
also				high				thought			
always				I'm				through			
any				inside				today			
around				jumped				together			
ask				knew				told			
asked				know				tries			
before				leave				turn			
began				might				turned			
being				morning				under			
below				much				until			
better				near				upon			
between				never				used			
both				number				walk			
brought				often				walked			
can't				only				walking			
change				opened				watch			
coming				other				where			
didn't				outside				while			
different				place				without			
does				right				woke			
don't				round				woken			
during				second				write			
every				show				year			
first				sometimes				young			
following				started							
found				still							

Name _____ Date _____

My Target Words

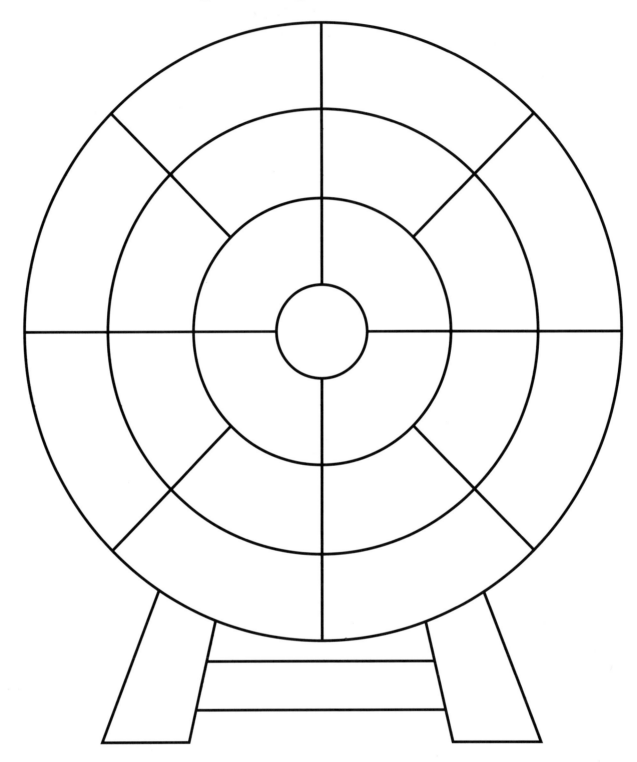

Over the next_____

I want to be able to read, write and spell these words.

Signed _____

does goes tries

Complete the
word cross

2 Look carefully at the spelling of does, goes and tries. Read this and underline where they are not spelt correctly.

When Susan dose the shopping she always gos to the same shops. She trys to go down the list and deos not miss anything. Firstly, she gose to the green-grocers. She trys to get there before it is busy. He really dus sell fresh vegetables. Next, she gows to the bakers. Great, he dos have her favourite cakes. Lastly, Susan trys the flower shop but duz not know what to choose.

Now write the passage correctly below..

_____

_____

_____

_____

_____

_____

_____

3 Find words which rhyme with tries.

lies   flies   dries   fries   pose   please   fleas   pies   spies   cries

tries
....

....

....

....

4 Using your dictionary and reading book, collect words with - **ie** - on the back of this sheet.

Where does the frog hang his coat?

In the croakroom!

knew   know   write

1   Put in the missing letters. Write the word in joined writing below.

...... ne......   .... ow   .... ite   .... ew   k ...... o ......   wr ....

....

2   Write these sentences spelling **knew**, **know** and **write** correctly.

(a)   The boy new all his tables and he could right them down.

....

(b)   "Right me a story but not one I already no, " said Mr. Smith.

....

(c)   We now how to rite a letter properly.

....

(d)   If you right the list down I will no what you want.

....

(e)   We new that you no my Gran.

....

(f)   Rite me a postcard so that I no how you are.

....

3   Find **knew, know** and **write**. How many? [ ]

o	k	n	e	w	e	k	k	n	o
k	n	o	w	k	w	n	n	n	n
n	e	w	r	o	n	o	o	o	o
o	w	r	i	t	e	e	w	o	w
w	k	i	t	w	w	w	w	e	w
w	e	n	e	o	r	r	r	o	i
r	k	k	o	w	r	i	i	e	t
i	n	n	e	w	r	i	t	e	e
t	o	e	e	r	i	t	e	e	w
k	n	o	w	w	r	i	t	e	r

4   Using your dictionary, find more words which begin with '**kn**' and '**wr**' (Use the back of this sheet if you do not have enough space).

kn ....

....

....

....

....

....

wr ....

....

....

....

....

....

Knock knock

Who's there?   Robin

Robin who?

Robin a bank to get rich!

Name _____ Date _____

 ,  ,  ,  ,

does	goes	tries	knew	know	write

started   stopped

1 Correct these words and write them below in joined writing.

startid   stoped   stated   stoppd   starrted   stopet

....

2 Find the correct ending for each sentence.

(a) The car started at the   but I found my maths hard.
(b) We stopped P.E.   stepped on to the platform.
(c) I started to unwrap   because it was raining.
(d) They stopped the race   first turn of the key.
(e) I started my homework   as the lesson was over.
(f) When the train stopped they   my Christmas presents.

Write the sentences correctly here.

(a) ....

(b) ....

(c) ....

(d) ....

(e) ....

(f) ....

3 Some words just add **ed** to make new words e.g. play, play**ed**.
Usually, after a single vowel and consonant at the end of a word, the last letter doubles then add **ed**. If there are two consonants at the end, then just add **ed**. Remember, a consonant is any letter which is not a, e, i, o, u. For example, tip - tipped, but park - parked.

(a) mark ....
(b) flip ....
(c) help ....
(d) chat ....
(e) blink ....

(g) pop ....
(h) lift ....
(i) hop ....
(j) bat ....
(k) part ....

Alec, how did your clothes get torn?

Oh, who?

4 Now, using your reading book, collect more words ending in **ed**.
Use the back of the sheet if you do not have enough space.

I stopped a boy getting beaten up

Me!

....

....

....

didn't don't can't I'm

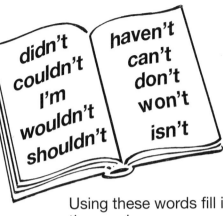

didn't
couldn't
I'm
wouldn't
shouldn't

haven't
can't
don't
won't
isn't

Using these words fill in the word sums.

1 **Didn't** is did not; **don't** is do not; **can't** is cannot; **I'm** is I am; but they are shortened. These are called contractions.

didn't = did + not _____ = _____ + _____

_____ = _____ + _____   _____ = _____ + _____

_____ = _____ + _____   _____ = _____ + _____

_____ = _____ + _____   _____ = _____ + _____

_____ = _____ + _____   _____ = _____ + _____

2 Look carefully at the spelling of didn't, don't, can't and I'm in these sentences. Now write them correctly. Use the spellings from the top of the page.

a) Ime going to Tom's party but I cannt go to Ben's.

_____

b) They didunt go to tennis as they cant play that game.

_____

c) I did'nt do my maths homework as I dont know how.

_____

d) As Im short of money, I ca'nt go to the shop.

_____

e) We do'nt sing and we cannt play anything.

_____

f) As Ime unwell, I didunt have any tea.

_____

3 Follow the snail trail and colour **didn't, don't, can't** and **I'm** where they are spelt correctly.

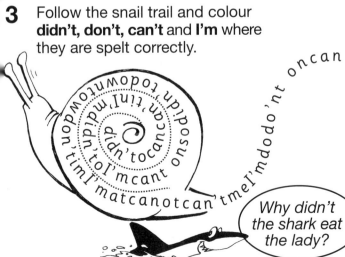

Why didn't the shark eat the lady?

It was a man-eating shark!

4 Now, using your reading book, collect together as many different shortened words or contractions as you can. Use the back of the sheet if necessary.

_____

_____

_____

_____

_____

_____

page 9

Name _____ Date _____

 ,  ,  ,

started	stopped	didn't	don't	can't	I'm

Proof Reading

Read the story carefully. Some of the words are not spelt correctly. The words in the top box will help you. Underline the mistakes and then write it as it should have been written.

does goes tries knew know write started
stopped didn't don't can't I'm

One day my teacher said "Ime going to ask you to right a story. I no how good you are at it. Today, I do'nt just want a story, Im hoping you'll rite a conversation."

I new all about speech marks but I dident no what to rite about. I just couldn't get startted.

"I just ca'nt think!" I said to myself. "Excuse me Miss. Dus it have to be a long story? I've had four trys but it just gose wrong!"

Miss Smith said, "Why do'nt you rite me one of your jokes Sam. Once you've startd them you cannt be stoped!"

This is what I wrote...

A lady gose into a pet shop and said, "Ime looking for a kitten going cheap."

The shopkeeper said, "We do'nt have one. Ours gose miaow!"

walk walked walking coming

1 Sort out these words. Write them in joined writing below.

lawk   gonimc   dlakew   ngwakli

....

---

2 Re-arrange these sentences so that the story makes sense.

We walked for half an hour.
"Are you coming for a walk?" said Dad.
Coming back we walked home via the sweet shop!
"We'll walk down to the woods," said Dad.
"Yes," I said, "Where are you walking to?"

---

3 Find **walk**, **walked**, **walking** and **coming**.
How many altogether?

a	w	a	l	k	e	d	a	w	a
w	a	l	k	e	w	a	l	a	k
a	l	w	a	l	k	a	n	l	c
l	k	w	a	l	k	e	d	k	o
k	i	a	c	l	l	n	k	i	m
i	n	c	n	o	k	l	o	n	i
n	g	k	c	o	m	i	n	g	n
g	o	c	o	m	l	i	n	g	g
a	c	o	m	i	n	g	n	g	w
c	o	m	e	w	a	l	k	g	o

4 Make a collection of as many movement words as possible e.g. **jump**, **slide**, **slither**, etc.

....

....

....

....

You were a long time coming. Didn't you hear me shout?

No Mum! Not till you shouted for the 6th time!

began being

1 Complete the word cross

2 Find **began** and **being**

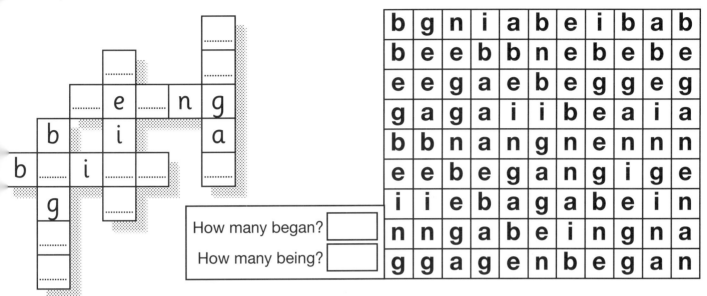

b	g	n	i	a	b	e	i	b	a	b
b	e	e	b	b	n	e	b	e	b	e
e	e	g	a	e	b	e	g	g	e	g
g	a	g	a	i	i	b	e	a	i	a
b	b	n	a	n	g	n	e	n	n	n
e	e	b	e	g	a	n	g	i	g	e
i	i	e	b	a	g	a	b	e	i	n
n	n	g	a	b	e	i	n	g	n	a
g	g	a	g	e	n	b	e	g	a	n

How many began? ☐

How many being? ☐

---

3 Find the correct ending for each sentence and join with a pencil line.

(a) Being a good runner,   it was sent outside.
(b) We began our holiday   and could not put it down.
(c) Being a 'Good Samaritan',   over which present to choose.
(d) They began to argue   you help other people.
(e) As the dog was being naughty,   Sam won the race.
(f) I began to read the book   by swimming in the pool.

Doctor, lately I began to think I was a pair of curtains.

Pull yourself together, Madam.

Write the sentences here.

(a) _____

(b) _____

(c) _____

(d) _____

(e) _____

(f) _____

---

4 Using your dictionary, check the spelling of these words.

a becose _____

b bettwen _____

c beyonde _____

d begining _____

e bewear _____

5 How many words, of two letters or more, can you make from **began** and **begin**.
Write on the back of the sheet.

Name .... Date ....

watch change

1 Look in the word bag. Find words from these 'word families'.

-tch	-nge
watch	change
....	....
....	....
....	....
....	....
....	....
....	....

Word bag words: strange, patch, manger, punch, much, ranger, match, batch, catch, range, hatch, latch, dagger, sang, stranger, danger

I'm going to change my mind.

Do you think that the new one will work any better!

2 Sort out these sentences. They must begin with a capital letter and end with a full stop.

(a) our favourite on T.V. programme we watch

....

(b) school and change from come home I my jeans into

....

(c) watch they the visitors to arrive for

....

(d) your socks!" change "go and said Mum

....

(e) go to we the cinema films watch to

....

(f) a butterfly in time will change a caterpillar into

....

3 Put in the missing letters.

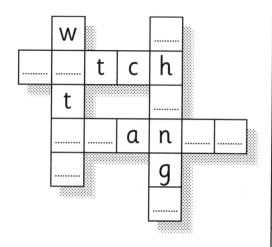

4 Find **change** and **watch**. How many?: **change** [　　]

How many?: **watch** [　　]

c	e	c	h	a	n	g	e	w
h	h	h	a	w	e	w	c	w
a	w	a	t	a	a	a	h	a
n	a	n	n	e	w	t	a	t
g	t	g	e	g	a	c	c	c
e	c	e	w	o	e	h	n	h
w	h	w	a	t	c	h	e	w
a	n	e	c	h	a	n	g	e

5

How many words, of two letters or more, can you make from **watch** and **change**.

Write on the back of this sheet.

Name .... Date ....

 ,  ,  ,  ,

walk	coming	began	being	watch	change

Name .... Date ....

brought   thought   think

1   Put in the missing letters, then write the word in joined writing below.

thi_ _   th_ _ght   brou_ _ _   thou_ _ _   b_ _ _ght

....

2   Make new words.

th
dr
s
w   ink   think ....
l   ....
p   ....
                                   ....
                                   ....

br
b
th   ought   ....
s   ....
f   ....
                                   ....
                                   ....

3   Find the correct ending for each sentence and join with a pencil line.

(a)   I thought carefully about   say anything."
(b)   We think our teacher   the birthday card.
(c)   The postman brought   with the word brought.
(d)   The florist brought   the right present to give.
(e)   The word thought rhymes   a bunch of flowers
(f)   Dad said, "Think before you   is wonderful!

Now write the sentences out here.

(a) ....

(b) ....

(c) ....

(d) ....

(e) ....

(f) ....

4   Using your reading book, make a collection of words ending in -**ght.** Use the back of this page if necessary.

....

....

....

....

Doctor, doctor, I think I am losing my mind!

Don't worry, you won't miss it!

Name .... Date ....

ask   asked   used   jumped

1 Sort out these words, then write them in joined writing on the line below.

desu   pdmeuj   kas   dsake

....

_____

2 Check the spelling of ask, asked, use, used and jumped in these sentences.
Write each sentence out correctly.

(a) The man askt if he could yous the phone.

....

(b) The rabbit jumpt out of the hedge onto the road.

....

(c) The boy askd his Mum if she had yousd her present.

....

(d) "Where is your dog?" askd Tom. "It jumpd the fence and ran away," said Ben.

....

....

(e) I will aske my Mum if I can come.

....

_____

3 Find **ask**, **asked**, **used** and **jumped**.

a	k	a	s	k	a	s	k	e	d
a	s	s	a	j	u	m	p	e	d
j	e	k	u	s	s	s	e	a	j
u	u	s	e	m	e	u	e	p	u
m	a	m	a	d	d	s	a	d	m
p	a	s	p	u	z	e	s	a	p
e	m	e	k	e	s	d	k	s	e
d	a	s	k	m	d	e	e	k	d
u	a	s	a	s	k	e	d	e	a
u	s	e	d	j	u	m	p	e	d

4 Think of other words with these endings.
(Use the back of this page if necessary).

___ ask   ___ se   ___ mp

....

....

....

....

....

Can I ask you something? Where do armies live?

Up the sleeves of your jacket.

Name _____   Date _____

 ,  ,  ,

brought	thought	think	ask	used	jumped

Proof Reading

Read the story carefully. Some of the words are not spelt correctly. The words in the top box will help you. Underline the mistakes and then write it as it should have been written.

know   started   stopped   didn't   don't   I'm
walk   walked   walking   coming   began
being   watch   change   brought   bought
think   ask   asked   used   jumped

One day I dident no what to do. I decided to go for a wark. I askt my friend Ben if he was cuming too. We beegan by warking into the woods. I stopt to tie my shoelace. Ben was beeing silly! He hid, then jumpt out at me.

"Have you brote any sweets?" I askt. "Yes," said Ben, "I bort them yesterday but downt fink you're having any! Ime eating them all!"

We walkt on and found a huge chestnut tree. "Wotch out, a conker is about to fall on your head." I shouted.

I starrtd to collect big conkers. I yoused a stick and got the biggest ones. I thought I would asc Ben if he'd chaynge some conkers for a sweet. I was right, he did!

opened turn turned

1 Put in the missing letters, then write the word in joined writing below.

t__ned   op____   tu__   __en__   turn__   o____d

....

---

2 Sort out these sentences. They must begin with a capital letter and end with a full stop.

(a)   the handle and I turned opened the door

....

(b)   you a present excited you open when feel

....

(c)   pass the parcel we must when playing take turns

....

(d)   go out the window never and leave open

....

(e)   frying pan turned over I in the the bacon

....

(f)   to play my is it turn

....

4 Find **open, opened, turn** and **turned**. How many altogether? [   ]

o	p	e	n	t	u	r	n	e	d
o	t	u	t	u	o	p	e	n	u
p	p	t	u	r	n	u	e	e	t
e	p	e	r	n	t	u	r	t	u
n	e	o	n	o	u	u	o	u	r
e	o	p	e	n	r	o	r	r	n
d	o	e	d	o	o	p	e	n	o
o	p	n	o	p	e	e	n	e	p
r	e	n	t	u	r	n	e	d	e
n	n	o	p	e	n	e	d	r	n

fur
happen curl wooden
even risen
burn church over burst
hurt
listen

ur   en

turn   open

3

Look in the chest and find words that belong to these families. Can you add more to the list? Use the back of this sheet if necessary.

....

....

....

....

....

It's our turn to have Mother for dinner dear.

I'd rather have fish and chips!.

leave   heard

1 Put in the missing letters.

l	__	__	v	e
	e			
h	e	a	__	__
		__		
h	__	__	r	d

2 Read the story carefully. **Leave** and **heard** may not be spelt correctly. Underline where they are spelt wrongly and then write it out correctly below.

One day when I was staying in my Auntie's big, old house, I herd a strange noise. I decided to leeve my bedroom and stand on the landing.

I herd it again. Yes, sure enough, I herd it again! "I must leave quickly, I think I have herd a burglar," I thought to myself. "Worse still, it might be a ghost who won't leeve my Auntie alone." I crept down to the hall and saw my Auntie's cat was just leaving!

....

....

....

....

....

....

....

3 Find **leave** and **heard**.

How many **leave**? ▢

How many **heard**? ▢

l	a	l	e	a	v	e	h	h	l
e	l	h	h	l	l	h	e	a	e
a	e	e	e	h	e	r	a	r	a
v	a	e	a	e	a	a	r	e	v
h	v	r	r	v	v	h	v	h	e
h	e	a	r	d	e	e	l	e	h
a	h	a	d	a	l	a	e	a	e
r	a	r	r	e	e	r	a	r	a
h	e	a	r	d	a	d	v	d	r
e	h	l	e	a	v	e	e	r	d

4 Using your reading book make a collection of words which have '**ea**' in the middle. (Use the back of this sheet if necessary).

....

....

....

....

....

Have you heard about the witch who looked in the mirror?

It was a shattering experience!

Name _____   Date _____

found   told

1 Find words which rhyme with found and told.

scold
ground
sound
gold bold
cold mound hold
sold fold round
hound
bound pound

Then put them in the correct kite.

found

told

2 Find the right ending for each sentence and join with a pencil line.

(a) We found money in the street   we told the teacher.
(b) I told my friend about the book   so we gave it to the police.
(c) They found a lost dog and took it   I was reading.
(d) My friend made me laugh   to the R.S.P.C.A.
(e) When we found the hamster   with old.
(f) The word told rhymes   when he told me a joke.

Sorry sir, we're out of flies today.

Waiter, waiter. I've found a beetle in my soup

Copy each sentence in the space below.

(a) ....

(b) ....

(c) ....

(d) ....

(e) ....

(f) ....

---

3 Colour **found** and **told** in the snake.

4 Using your reading book and dictionary make a collection of words with '**ou**' and '**ld**' in them. (Use the back of this page if necessary).

....

....

....

....

Name _____ Date _____

 ,  ,  ,

opened	turn	leave	heard	found	told

Name ....   Date ....

gone woke woken

1 Put in the missing letters.

```
              w         g
              o
        o     e   n
        o           e
   w    k
 g    n
       n
 e
```

2 Put **gone**, **woke** or **woken** in the gaps.

One day I .... up with tooth-ache. I hoped it would soon be ...., but I had .... up in terrible pain.

"Has it ....?" asked Mum. "No, it's just the same as when I .... up," I replied.

Mum took me to the dentist and now it has .... In fact I've never .... up with tooth-ache since!

3 Sort out the sentences. They must begin with a capital letter and end with a full stop.

(a) to sleep in its cot the baby gone has

....

(b) up early we woke morning in the

....

(c) was woken Mum by a noise strange

....

(d) gone to on holiday France they have

....

(e) to the sound woke I birds singing of

....

(f) for school!" woken was I by Mum shouting, late "You're

....

o	g	o	n	e	n	w	o	k	e	n
w	e	n	o	g	o	o	g	o	n	e
o	w	w	w	o	w	o	k	e	n	e
k	w	o	e	n	g	g	w	w	o	w
e	o	k	k	e	n	o	w	o	k	o
n	w	e	o	e	o	g	n	k	k	k
g	o	n	e	w	n	o	o	e	w	e
o	k	g	o	n	e	n	w	n	o	o
n	e	w	k	w	o	w	o	k	e	g

4 Find **gone**, **woke** and **woken**.
How many of each?

gone [   ]   woke [   ]   woken [   ]

5

Using your reading book and dictionary collect words ending in **-ke** and **-en**. List them on the back of this sheet.

Doctor, My husband woke up this morning and thinks he is a rubber band!

Tell him to snap out of it.

© Topical Resources. May be photocopied for classroom use only.

might show

1   Write the missing letters. Then write the words in joined writing below.

mi.....t   .....ow   m.....t   sh.....   mig.....   s.....w

....

2

| right | flow |
| sight | low |
| tight |
| night | blow |
| row |
| flight | sow | light |
| glow | grow | fight |

Find words that rhyme with.

might ....

....

....

....

....

show ....

....

....

....

3   Write these sentences spelling **might** and **show** correctly.

(a) We miyt be able to go to the horse sho.

....

(b) If you showe me, then I miyte be able to knit.

....

(c) I will showe you the way to the office.

....

(d) We miyt be going to Spain this year.

....

(e) Show me the photo, as I miyt know your friend.

....

(f) 'Miyte' rhymes with 'night' and 'showe' rhymes with 'flow'.

s	h	o	w	m	s	s	i	t	m
h	o	m	o	i	s	h	o	w	i
o	m	i	w	g	h	o	o	e	g
m	i	g	h	t	o	w	s	w	h
i	g	h	s	m	i	g	h	t	t
g	h	t	h	i	i	s	h	o	w
h	t	o	o	g	m	g	o	l	s
t	o	w	w	m	i	g	h	t	h
o	s	h	o	w	g	o	i	t	o
m	i	g	h	t	h	s	h	o	w

4 Find **might** and **show**.
How many **might**? ☐
How many **show**? ☐

5 Make a collection of words with **ow** and **ight** at the end. (Use the back of this sheet if necessary).

....

....

....

....

What might a policeman say to the man with three heads?

"'Allo, 'allo, 'allo!"

page 25

almost   always

1 Put in the missing letters. Then write the word below in joined writing.

a mo........   al ...... y...   ......most   ......ways   ......most

....

2 Find the right endings for each sentence.

Why are elephants always grey?

So that they can't be mistaken for raspberries!

(a) We almost always go to   on Sundays.
(b) They always have fish   in the sky at night.
(c) I have almost finished my   France on holiday.
(d) It is almost one month   and chips on Friday.
(e) We always go to church   maths homework.
(f) There are almost always stars   until Christmas.

(a) ....

(b) ....

(c) ....

(d) ....

(e) ....

(f) ....

3 Using your dictionary, complete these words which begin with **al**

al..og..t.....r

als....

alr.....dy

althou........

alm.gh........

alt....rn..tiv.....

4

Find **almost** and **always** and colour them.

5 Make a collection of words which end in **st** or **ay** and list them on the back of this sheet.
Use your reading book and dictionary to help you.

Name _____ Date _____

 ,  ,  ,

gone	woke	might	show	almost	always

Proof Reading

Read the story carefully. Some of the words are not spelt correctly. The words in the top box will help you. Underline the mistakes and then write it as it should have been written.

> **told, found, heard, leave, turn, opened, always, almost, show, might, woke, gone, I'm, didn't, started, change, watch, thought, jumped, walked, coming, began, knew, goes, think**

I wok up and jumpt out of bed. I new it was Sport's Day! I herd Mum - allmost certainly she was making breakfast.

"I'me cuming to woch today. You allways win a race!" she said.

"I miyte not Mum. I thinc Pam miyt chanj all that. Ime tolled she gose like lightening! She'll leeve me behind!" I replied.

I walkt to school and fownd Pam was as excited as I was. "I'll showe her," I thawt.

However, things dident go as I thort. It beegan to tern from sunshine to rain. The heavens opend and my chance of winning was gon. The race dident even get starrted!

Name .... Date ....

only any

1

Put in the missing letters.

2 Write these sentences spelling **only** and **any** correctly.

a Have you eney sweets?

....

b I have ownley one brother.

....

c We onlee go swimming once a week.

....

d Eneybody can come to my party.

....

e Stephen is an onlee child. He doesn't have eney brothers or sisters.

....

f Onlee children who have eney singing lessons can join the choir.

....

3 Sort out these muddled words; they all have **any**, in them. Write them in joined writing below.

yamn   ydanboy   neonya   thgniyna   eerhwyan

....

4 Find **any and only**. How many **any**? ☐ How many **only**? ☐

o	n	l	y	o	n	o	o	n	l	a
o	a	n	y	a	l	a	n	y	a	n
n	n	a	n	y	o	n	l	l	o	y
l	y	l	o	o	n	l	y	a	y	n
y	n	a	y	n	l	a	l	a	n	o
a	n	o	n	l	y	n	a	n	y	n
a	n	y	l	y	o	y	n	y	a	l
a	n	o	n	o	n	l	y	a	n	y
a	n	y	l	o	n	l	y	n	y	a

5 Make a collection of words ending in -**ly** and -**ny** on the back of this sheet. Use your reading book and dictionary to help you.

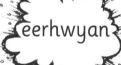

Baa, Baa, Black Sheep,
Have you any wool?
Yes sir, Yes sir,
Three bags full.
One for the master,
And one for little Jenny,
And one for Mrs Winterbottom.
So you're not getting any!

never every

1 Put in the missing letters, then write the word below in joined writing.

n..v..r   ev..r....   ... ...ver   ev... ..y   n... ...r   ... ...ry

....

---

2 Read this carefully. **Never** and **every** are spelt wrongly.
Underline the mistakes then write it correctly.

Evree week we go swimming. We nevur miss. Evrebody in my family can swim and have nevur had any difficulties. Really, evreyone should learn to swim. Evreewhere we go on holiday, we nevur fail to hear of accidents in the water. It would nevur happen if everione learnt to swim.

....

....

....

....

....

---

3 Sort out these muddled words. They all have **ever** or **every** in them.
Write them in joined writing below.

evowher   neoreyev   ryveedyob   hwreeryeev   yignthreev

....

---

4 Find **never** and **every** in the snake and colour them in.

5 Make a collection of words that end in -**er** on the back of this sheet.
Use you reading book and dictionary to help you.

What fruit is never lonely?

Pears!

number   second

1   Sort out these words. Write them in joined writing below.

oncdes   mbuner   coesnd   bremun

....

2   Find the correct ending for each sentence and join with a pencil line. Then write them below.

(a)   There are sixty seconds   are all even.
(b)   The number after ninty-nine   second in the race.
(c)   On Sports Day Tom was   he got a toy car.
(d)   On their second attempt, the climbers   in a minute.
(e)   On our side of the street the house numbers   is one hundred.
(f)   For the little boy's second birthday   made it to the top.

(a) ....

(b) ....

(c) ....

(d) ....

(e) ....

(f) ....

3   Find **number** and **second**.

How many **number**? ☐

How many **second**? ☐

n	u	m	s	e	c	o	n	d	o
u	n	h	e	s	n	n	u	s	s
m	u	u	u	o	o	u	m	e	e
b	m	b	c	m	s	m	b	c	c
s	b	m	n	e	b	b	e	n	o
s	e	c	o	n	d	e	r	u	n
o	r	c	d	s	e	r	r	m	d
s	e	c	o	n	d	r	e	b	o
n	u	m	b	n	u	m	b	e	r
s	e	c	o	n	d	e	e	r	s

4   Find a word or words with **second** in, which matches each meaning. Use your dictionary to help you.

(a)   A school for children over eleven.

....

(b)   Not new.

....

(c)   Being able to see into the future.

....

(d)   Not of the best quality.

....

Add these numbers; 28, 69, 43 and then multiply by 65. What do you get?

The wrong answer!

28 + 69 + 43 =

5

Write the numbers to twenty in words.

Check your spelling in the dictionary.

 ,  ,  ,

only	any	never	every	number	second

often   suddenly

1 Put in the missing letters, then write the words below in joined writing.

of....n   su....enly   ....en   ....dden....   of....n

....

2 Write these sentences spelling **suddenly** and **often** correctly.

a Jack ofen goes to the swimming pool on Sunday.

....

b Dad sudenly decided we would go on holiday.

....

c On Saturday Mum ofen bakes.

....

d Sudenley, at the end of the match, a goal was scored.

....

e Offen, when you are in the country, you suddenlee see a rabbit.

....

3 **Often** and **sudden** end in **en**.
Sort out these mixed up words
which also end in **en**

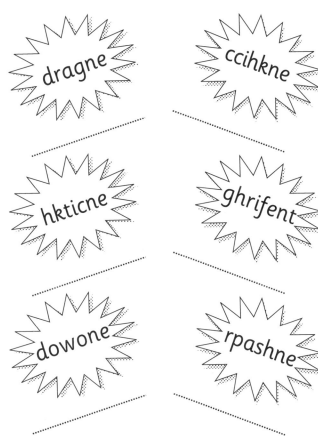

dragne

ccihkne

hkticne

ghrifent

dowone

rpashne

s	o	s	u	d	d	e	n	l	y	s
u	s	u	d	d	e	n	l	y	s	u
d	u	u	e	o	o	o	o	s	u	d
d	d	o	d	n	f	f	f	u	d	d
e	d	s	o	d	t	t	t	d	d	e
n	e	o	f	t	e	n	e	e	e	n
l	n	n	o	f	n	n	n	n	n	l
y	l	o	f	t	e	n	l	l	l	y
o	y	t	o	f	t	e	n	y	y	o

4

Find **often** and **suddenly**.

What are baby witches often good at in school?

Spelling!

5

Use the letters in **often** and **suddenly** and make as many words of two letters or more that you can.

List them on the back of this sheet.

Name .... Date ....

until   upon

1   Put in the missing letters, then write the words below in joined writing.

un............   up..........   ....til   ... .on   u l   u ..... n

....

---

2   Find the right ending for these sentences.

(a) We waited until four o'clock   landed on the roof.

(b) The story began with   until nine o'clock.

(c) You do not go to high school   upon the runway.

(d) The aeroplane landed   for the bus to come.

(e) We stayed up   until you are eleven.

(f) The bird flew down and   "Once upon a time".

Now, write them here.

(a) ....

(b) ....

(c) ....

(d) ....

(e) ....

(f) ....

3

Put in the missing letters.

---

4 Find **upon** and **until**.

How many **upon**? ☐

How many **until**? ☐

u	p	o	n	p	u	n	y	p	o	n
t	u	n	t	i	l	u	p	o	n	u
u	n	p	o	t	u	p	o	n	o	p
n	t	i	o	u	n	u	n	t	i	l
t	i	t	i	n	t	u	n	o	p	u
i	l	u	n	t	i	l	u	t	o	p
l	i	p	o	i	l	p	o	n	i	o
o	n	o	p	l	u	u	n	t	i	l
n	i	n	i	u	p	o	n	u	n	t

5   Make as many words, of two or more letters, from the words **until** and **upon**.

List them on the back of this sheet.

Why are you standing upon your head, Bill?

I'm just turning things over in my mind!

sometimes   better

1   Put in the missing letters, then write the word in joined writing below.

so.......ti....s   be....er   some......es   b.......r

....

---

2   Sort out these sentences. They must all begin with a capital letter and end with a full stop.

(a) have we tea for pizza sometimes

....

(b) better Maths P.E. like I than

....

(c) go to my Aunt sometimes with we stay

....

(d) asked, Mum "Do feel better?" you

....

(e) with on holiday sometimes we our friends go

....

(f) we the teacher better tell had that over fallen has Pat

....

---

3   Here are some words which begin with **some**.
The endings are muddled up.
Sort them out.

1   some (stiem) = sometimes

2   some (eerhw) = ...

3   some (neo) = ...

4   some (ngiht) = ...

5   some (woh) = ...

6   some (ydob) = ...

4   Think of more words which end in **er**.
Use your dictionary and reading book to help you.
Use the back of this sheet if necessary.

--er words

better............   ....

....

....

....

....

....

....

....

....

Doctor, Sometimes I think I'm a spoon.

Stay quiet and don't stir yourself

Name .... Date ....

 ,  ,  ,

often	suddenly	until	upon	sometimes	better

Proof Reading

Read the story carefully. Some of the words are not spelt correctly. The words in the top box will help you. Underline the mistakes and then write it as it should have been written.

---

suddenly, until, upon, sometimes, better,
only, any, never, every, number, second,
woke, open, heard, found, told, thought,
thinking, jumped, often, coming, began,
opened, watched, stopped, knew, don't

"There is nevur enything exciting happens to me," I thort to myself.

Sudenlee I herd a loud bang. I stopt playing and jumpt over the garden wall. There I fownd two cars had crashed. I opend a car door and new the driver was hurt.

"Evree secund matters! I'd bettur go and get Mum," I was thincking to myself.

I beegan knocking uppon our door and wock Mum, who was asleep. She tolled the police and onlee minutes later an ambulance was cuming down the road. We wotched with a numbur of others untill it sped away.

"Sumtimes it is betur not to wish for exciting things. I hope they dont happen oftun!'

Name .... Date ....

during morning today

1 Sort out the words. Then write them in joined writing below.

gnnirom   riudng   adoty   mnronig   rudngi

....

2 Read this carefully. **During, morning** and **today** are spelt wrongly. Underline the mistakes then write it out correctly.

This morrning our teacher said, "Todday, durring the morrning, we will have some visitors." At morening play a large van arrived. A policeman got out and said, "Tooday we have brought some of our horses and durinng the next lesson this morening we will talk to you about them."

It was the best morrning in school we had ever had!

....

....

....

....

....

....

3 Find **during**, **morning** and **today**.

t	t	u	m	t	o	d	a	y	d	u
o	o	m	o	r	n	i	n	g	d	r
d	d	u	r	i	n	g	m	t	u	m
a	u	d	n	m	d	d	o	o	r	o
y	r	u	i	o	u	u	r	d	i	r
m	o	r	n	i	n	g	r	a	n	n
t	o	i	g	r	o	t	n	i	g	i
c	a	n	t	o	d	a	y	n	n	n
y	o	g	o	r	d	u	r	i	n	g

4 Make a collection of day and night words. Check the spelling in your dictionary. (Use the back of this sheet if necessary.)

....

....

....

....

....

....

I'm afraid Pam won't be at school today

Who's calling?

It's my mother!

© Topical Resources. May be photocopied for classroom use only.

Name .... Date ....

first half

1   Put in the missing letters. Then copy the word below in joined up writing.

f......st   ha......   fir......   h......f   f......t   ......lf

....

---

2   Find the right ending for these sentences and join with a pencil line.

(a)   The first letter of the   to my friend.

(b)   Half a metre is   alphabet is 'a'.

(c)   The first day we go to school   the running race.

(d)   There are thirty minutes   fifty centimetres.

(e)   Robert came first in   is Monday.

(f)   I gave half of my sweets   in half an hour.

A large lady on the Rhine,
Was asked at what time
she would dine,
She said, "At seven,
And half past eleven,
With a snack at a quarter
to nine!".

(a) ....

(b) ....

(c) ....

(d) ....

(e) ....

(f) ....

---

3   Using your dictionary, find the missing letters in these place number words.

s......ond   f......rth   sev......n......

th......d   f......th   e......h..h

twe......th   n......th

4   Find **first** and **half** in the snake.

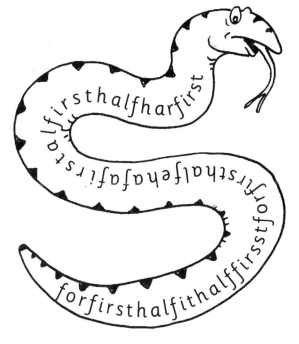

5   Using your dictionary and reading book, collect words with **-ir** in them, e.g. sh**ir**t.
Use the back of this sheet if necessary.

....

....

    page 39

Name .... Date ....

 ,  ,  ,

during	morning	today	first	half

Name .... Date ....

before   much

1   Sort out the words, then write them below in joined writing.

bferoe   cumh   fbeero   uchm   foebre   uhmc

....

2   Sort out these sentences.

(a) it is have we P.E. before maths

....

(b) the toy much how is the top shelf? on

....

(c) before hands your eating wash

....

(d) to do there so is much you when house! move

....

(e) I go before to bed my teeth I brush

....

(f) too much on my there was dinner plate

....

How much is a haircut? £2

How much is a shave? £1

Right, shave my head.

---

3   Find **before** and **much**.

How many **before**? ☐

How many **much**? ☐

e	b	e	f	o	r	e	m	u	c
b	e	f	o	r	e	a	m	b	b
e	o	o	m	u	c	h	u	e	e
f	b	r	m	u	c	h	c	m	f
o	b	e	m	o	c	e	h	u	o
r	o	b	f	u	e	h	o	c	r
e	b	e	f	o	r	e	m	h	e
w	e	f	e	f	r	f	u	b	o
e	w	o	w	e	r	e	c	e	r
b	e	f	o	r	e	w	h	f	e

4   These words all begin with **be**.
Use your dictionary to help find them

(to start)
be__n

(be part of)
bel__g

(watch out!)
bew__e

(in the middle of)
bet__e__n

(be good!)
beh__e

(have faith)
bel__v__

(at the back)
beh__d

(be disloyal)
betr____

5   Collect words that end in **ch**. Use you reading book and dictionary to help you.
(Use the back of this sheet if necessary).

still   while

3   Write these sentences spelling **still** and **while** correctly.

.....ill   whi.....   sti.....   .....ile   s.....ll   w.....e

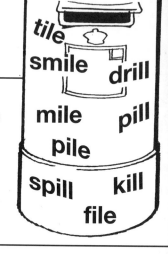

....

fill
tile
smile   drill
mile   pill
pile
spill   kill
file

3

Sort out the words which rhyme with **still** and **while**.

while   still

3   Write these sentences spelling **still** and **while** correctly.

(a) "Please stand stil wile I am speaking," said the teacher.

....

(b) Wile it was wet at playtime, the children got out the games.

....

(c) It is stil raining outside.

....

(d) "Wile you are working you may stil talk," said Mr Smith.

....

(e) They could stil see the mountain top wile it was foggy.

....

(f) Wile it was stil dark the thief climbed in the window.

....

4 Find **still** and **while** and colour them in.

sitstilwillwhilesillstillwhiletillsillstillwetewhilesitestill

Doctor, I still think I am a bee.

I've told you to buzz off.

5 Make a collection of words ending in **ll**. Use your reading book and dictionary to help you. Write on the back of this sheet.

year   young

1 Sort out the words and write them in joined writing below.

arey   yngou   yare   yuong   raey   gouyn

....

2 Find the right ending for each sentence.

a) A young cow is   months in a year.
b) The word year rhymes   to go to playschool.
c) The young child did not want   called a calf.
d) One hundred years   is young.
e) The opposite of old   makes a century.
f) There are twelve   with fear.

Now write them here.

a)

b)

c)

d)

e)

f)

3 Find **year** and **young**.

How many **year**? ☐ How many **young**? ☐

y	y	e	a	r	y	o	u	n	g
o	o	r	y	o	u	n	g	u	n
u	y	u	o	o	y	e	a	r	y
n	e	e	n	e	u	r	r	y	o
g	a	y	a	g	n	n	e	e	u
o	r	o	r	r	o	y	g	a	n
y	o	u	n	g	y	e	a	r	g
e	r	n	o	u	y	a	r	e	a
a	e	g	y	e	a	r	e	o	r
r	n	y	e	y	e	a	r	a	u

4 Make a collection of words with **-ear-** in them, e.g. hear.

Make a collection of words ending in **-ng**, e.g.long. (Use the back of this sheet if necessary).

....

....

....

....

....

There was a young man from Leek,
Who, instead of a nose, grew a beak.
It grew quite absurd,
Till he looked like a bird.
He migrates at the end of next week.

Name .... Date ....

 ,  ,  ,  , year , young

before	much	still	while	year	young

Proof Reading

Read the story carefully. Some of the words are not spelt correctly. The words in the top box will help you. Underline the mistakes and then write it as it should have been written.

> **turned, before, much, while, year, young, gone, during, morning, today, first, half, began, watched, suddenly, second, open, heard, walked, opened, leave, started, stopped, don't, can't, think, watched, thought, might, knew**

Beefor school this morrning, durring breakfast, we herd a noise in the living room. Suddenlee, it stopt. Harf a minute later it starrted again.

Dad warked into the living room and in a secund new what it was. On the furst bookshelf sat a yung bird. It cannt have been more than a yeer old.

It began to fly around the room. "Oh no!" I thort. "It miyte hurt itself!"

Then Dad had an idea as he wotched the bird. "It cannt get out. If we opun the window and leeve it alone it mite fly away."

Quickly, Dad opend a window and wile he turnd for a secund, the bird flew out and was gon!

We watcht it fly into the trees and new it was safe. I downt thinc we'll have mutch more excitment tooday!

Name .... Date ....

round around

1 Choose words from the circle which rhyme with round and around

round ....

around ....

....

Word circle: hand, mend, found, wound, mound, sand, bend, kind, sound, land, wind, grand, find, hound, rind, ground, pound, band, bound

2 Sort out these muddled sentences.

(a) Tom's I went house to my around friend

....

(b) found Ben on lying the pound ground a

....

(c) sound loud the made a bark the of grey-hound

....

(d) string the Susan wound ball of up

....

(e) of sand the children castle with the mound made a

....

(f) mine from Sam's the corner house is round

....

3 How many words that rhyme with **round** can you find? *Clue: the word may go along down or diagonally.*

f	h	m	a	r	o	u	n	d	p
s	o	v	o	o	b	p	t	o	o
t	u	u	s	u	f	o	u	n	u
n	n	l	n	n	n	n	u	b	n
d	d	r	e	d	d	g	n	d	d
s	o	u	n	d	w	o	u	n	d
a	m	o	u	n	d	s	a	t	o
s	a	g	r	o	u	n	d	e	n

Which word is there three times? ....

4 Make a collection of words ending in **nd**, using you reading book and dictionary to help you.
Write on the back of this sheet.

What is black and white and goes round and round?

A Zebra in a revolving door!

right   high

1 .Put in the missing letters

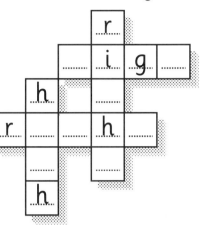

2 Add **-ight** to these letters to make new words.

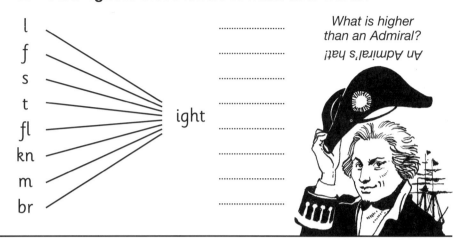

l
f
s
t
fl
kn
m
br

ight

....
....
....
....
....
....
....
....

What is higher than an Admiral?

An Admiral's hat!

2 Find the right ending for these sentences and join them with a pencil line. Then write them below.

(a) The teacher gave me full marks   on the shelf.
(b) The book is up high   the flame burns brightly.
(c) At the next turn on the right   high in the sky.
(d) The plane flew   about the bully.
(e) The boy was right to tell the teacher   is the supermarket.
(f) When the gas is on high   as my sums were all right.

(a) _____

(b) _____

(c) _____

(d) _____

(e) _____

(f) _____

3 Colour **right** and **high** in the snail trail.

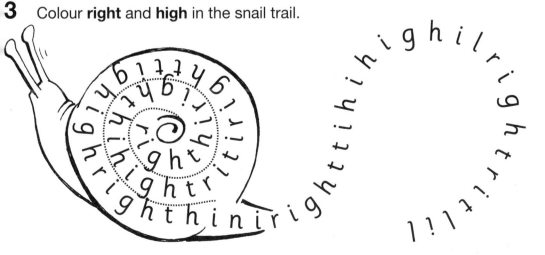

4

Draw your own wordsearch on the back of this sheet for the words **right** and **high**.

Try it out on a friend.

Name .... Date ....

other   under

1   Put in the missing letters then write the word below in joined writing.

o .... er   un ..... r   ..... t .. er   ..... der   o ..... r   u ..... r

....

2   Sort out these sentences. They must begin with a capital letter and end with a full stop.

(a) other we on went day school our trip the

....

(b) a hedgehog found we the under leaves

....

(c) the is Art I like but Maths subject other I enjoy

....

(d) was sheltered raining under a tree we because it

....

(e) my under pen dropped I the table

....

(f) a book fair other the week at school had we

....

3   Here are some more words which tell us about the position of things.
Use your dictionary to complete them.

ins ..... e   ag ..... n .. t

o ... ts ... d ...   am ..... g

ov .....   n ..... r

thr ..... gh   acr ..... s

ar ..... nd   ab .. v ...

4   Find **other** and **under**.

t	o	t	h	e	r	h	u	o	u
o	u	u	o	t	u	o	n	t	n
o	o	o	u	h	o	n	d	h	o
t	t	t	n	u	n	d	e	r	t
h	h	h	d	n	n	e	r	o	h
e	e	e	e	t	o	d	o	e	e
r	r	r	r	r	d	o	e	o	r
u	n	d	e	u	n	d	e	r	u
r	u	n	d	e	r	u	e	d	n
o	t	h	e	r	u	n	d	e	r

5   Make a collection of words ending in **er**. Use your reading book and dictionary to help you. Write on the back of this sheet.

The other night I dreamed I was sitting next to the most beautiful girl in the world.

Oh - what was I wearing?

Name _____ Date _____

 ,  ,  ,  ,

round	around	right	high	other	under

along across

1 Sort out these words, then write them below in joined writing.

orssca   gnola   rcosas   onlag   roscsa   goaln

....

2 Read this carefully. **Along** and **across** are spelt wrongly.
Underline the mistakes and then write it out correctly.

My parents took us allong to an adventure park. I walked acrross the ladders

on the climbing frame and then allong the narrow plank. My brother fell

as he went acros it. We walked back to the car accros the grass and allong

the path.

....

....

....

....

....

....

3 Find **along** and **across**.

a	a	c	r	o	s	s	a	a	c
a	l	o	a	n	g	a	l	r	o
c	o	o	s	a	c	r	o	s	s
a	n	a	n	n	r	o	n	a	s
l	g	l	c	g	g	s	g	c	a
o	o	a	c	r	o	s	s	r	l
n	a	l	o	n	o	l	o	o	o
g	r	a	c	r	o	s	s	s	n
a	c	r	o	s	s	o	s	s	g

4 Find other words which end in **-ng** or **-ss**.
Use the dictionary to help you and continue
your lists on the back of this sheet if
necessary.

-ng
thing

....

....

....

-ss
dress

....

....

....

I've come along because my husband thinks he's an elastic band

Tell him to snap out of it.

inside   outside

1 Put in the missing letters and then write the word in joined writing below.

in..... .....d.....   ....tsi.....   ....side   outs..... ....   in..... ..... e

....

---

2 Find the right ending for these sentences and join with a pencil line.

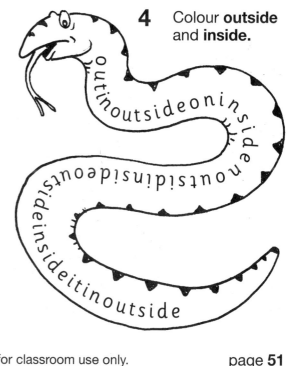

a)   The vicar waited   outside the shop.
b)   We played rounders   the front garden.
c)   The letter was inside   inside the boy's mouth.
d)   Outside our house is   inside the church.
e)   The dentist looked   outside, on the field.
f)   The vegetables were on display   a brown envelope.

Now write them below.

a) ....

b) ....

c) ....

d) ....

e) ....

f) ....

---

3 Using your dictionary
find more words which begin with:

in   **out**
invite   outing

....

....

....

....

4 Colour **outside**
and **inside**.

5 Draw your own wordsearch for inside and outside
on the back of this sheet.
Try it out on a friend.

also   such   both

1   Put in the missing letters, then write the word in joined writing below.

a ...s ...   su ....   bo ....so   ... ...ch   ... ...th

....

2   Sort out the sentences. They must begin with a capital letter and end with a full stop.

(a)   Easter it is and my birthday also is it

....

(b)   such a had we time good on holiday

....

(c)   went their Aunt to visit children both

....

(d)   come can to both you of tea

....

(e)   such was it film good a the cinema saw we at

....

(f)   sing not only she can she the piano play also can

....

3   Find **also**, **such** and **both**.

How many **such**? ☐

How many **also**? ☐

How many **both**? ☐

a	l	s	o	t	s	u	c	h	s
l	b	b	l	a	a	s	a	a	a
a	l	o	s	l	l	a	l	s	l
l	l	t	t	u	u	s	s	u	s
s	o	h	o	h	c	u	o	c	o
o	b	o	t	h	a	h	b	h	h
u	t	l	a	l	s	u	t	o	u
c	h	s	s	s	u	c	h	t	c
h	a	o	b	o	t	h	a	h	h

4 Find **also**, **such** and **both** in the snake.

Waiter, waiter, there's a bee in my alphabet soup!

I hope there's also a 'c' and an 'f' and lots of other letters as well.

5 make a collection of words that end in **th**.

Write on the back of this sheet.

alsobohlbothasuchalso
osuchasbowthalso
suchbothallsoibothsuchalso

Name .... Date ....

 ,  ,  ,  ,

along	across	inside	outside	also	such	both

Proof Reading

Read the story carefully. Some of the words are not spelt correctly. The words in the top box will help you. Underline the mistakes and then write it as it should have been written.

> **outside, don't, seconds, thought, also, such, under, think, right, ask, high, brought, jumped, along, across, asked, coming, inside, only, other, both, morning, told, asked**

The othur day it was suche lovely weather outsiyde, that Tom and I askt Dad if we could put up the tent.

"Yes! Its a lovely morrning," he said.

We bothe put it up undur the tree in the garden. In secunds we jumpt insiyde to check it was riyte. We thort it was. We went allong to asc Sam if he was cuming acros to play. We allso tolled Emma about it.

"Is it hiye enough to stand up in?" she askt

"I donnt thinc so! Its onlee one metre highe!" I replied.

We brote our lunch insiyde and we all thort it was wonderful!

below above between

Put in the missing letters, then write the word in joined writing below.

bel_____   ab_____e   betw_____n   _____low   _____ov_____   _____ween

_____   _____   _____   _____   _____

2 The words **below**, **above** and **between** have been used in the wrong place in this story. Find them and replace them with the right word.

One day I could not find my best pen. I looked between the chair and on the top shelf below my bed. I then looked above the pages of my car book. Mum suggested, "Look below the pages of your school books. It may be here!" Finally, bending down, I looked above my desk and there it was.

Now write the story correctly here.

_____

_____

_____

_____

_____

_____

3 Find **below, above** and **between**.

How many **below**? ☐
How many **above**? ☐
How many **between**? ☐

a	t	o	b	e	l	o	w	t	b	b
b	a	b	o	e	t	e	o	a	e	a
e	e	e	a	w	t	w	o	b	t	b
t	a	l	b	b	t	w	v	o	w	o
w	b	o	o	o	o	o	e	v	e	v
e	o	w	v	w	e	r	t	e	e	e
e	v	t	e	w	w	e	e	w	n	o
n	e	o	w	b	e	t	w	e	e	n
a	e	b	e	t	w	e	e	n	w	e

4 Using your dictionary, complete these words which begin with **be**.

ben_____th   (under)
bes_____d_____   (next to)
bew_____r_____   (watch out)
bey_____d   (out of reach)
bec_____se   (for the reason)

What is the difference between a buffalo and a bison?

Ever tried washing your hands in a Buffalo?

5 Draw a cartoon picture to show the meaning of **below**, **above** and **between** on the back of this sheet.

Name .... Date ....

through near

1 Put in the missing letters.

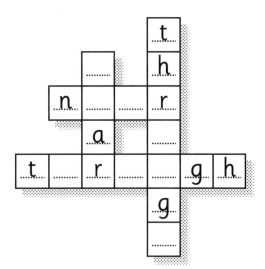

2 Find words that rhyme with **near** and have these meanings.

to listen ....   to be afraid ....

a weapon ....   to understand is to be ....

to cry or shed a ....   cut sheeps wool ....

3 Use **through** and **threw** in the gaps.

(a) I .... a ball for my dog.

(b) We walked .... long grass.

(c) I peeped .... the window.

(d) We .... a stone in the water.

(e) The boy .... a brick .... the window

(f) Look .... my homework, please.

4 Find the correct ending for each sentence and join with a pencil line.

(a) 'Alice through the looking   we saw a deer.

(b) We walk to school because   with fear.

(c) We couldn't see through the window   it bites!

(d) The word near rhymes   glass' is a book.

(e) While walking through the woods   we live nearby.

(f) Do not go near the dog because   as it was made of frosted glass.

Now write the sentences here.

(a) ....

(b) ....

(c) ....

(d) ....

(e) ....

(f) ....

5 Using your reading book collect words with **ea** in them. Write on the back of this sheet if necessary.

....

....

....

What did the pipeline shout through to the drill?

Oil be seeing you.

Name .... Date ....

 ,  ,  ,

below	above	between	through	near

following where place

1 Put in the missing letters, then write the word in joined writing below.

fo___o___ing   ___ere   pla___   f___ow___g   whe___   p___ce

....

---

2 Sort these words into the right word family

race
bellow face
space mellow
grace trace wallow
swallow
hollow

follow

place

3 Sort out these sentences. They must all begin with a capital letter and end with a full stop.

(a) was master its the dog following

....

(b) find I head-teacher? the will where

....

(c) where the we place born visited was the poet

....

(d) following the journey were we on map the

....

(e) badgers know I where a place live

....

4 Find **following**, **where** and **place**.

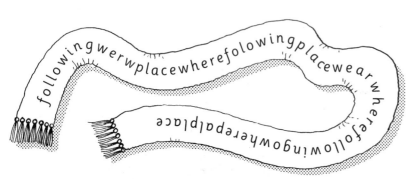

Where do birds meet for coffee?   In a Nest-café

5

Use the letters in **following**, **where** and **place** to make words of two letters or more.
Write on the back of this sheet.

different   without

Look carefully at each word. It is spelt incorrectly. Write it correctly in joined writing below.

liferent   withot   differrent   withuot   diffrent

....

2   Find the right ending for these sentences and join with a pencil line.

a)   The boy spelt 'different'   not the same.
b)   Tom looked in his pocket   as shout.
c)   In P.E. we can choose   he had come without his glasses.
d)   Mr Smith could not see as   without two 'f's'.
e)   The word different means   and found he had come without money.
f)   Without has the same ending   different activities.

Now write them here.

a) ....

b) ....

c) ....

d) ....

e) ....

f) ....

3   Find **different** and **without**.

d	o	u	w	i	t	h	o	u	t	d
i	d	i	f	f	e	r	e	n	t	i
f	e	i	w	i	t	h	o	u	t	f
f	d	i	f	f	e	r	e	n	t	f
e	w	i	t	h	o	u	t	e	e	e
r	t	o	w	i	t	h	o	u	t	r
e	e	d	i	f	f	e	r	e	n	e
n	w	i	t	h	o	u	t	o	u	n
t	o	w	i	t	h	o	u	t	e	t

4   Make a collection of words with '**ou**' in them, using your reading book. Write on the back of the sheet if necessary.

....

....

....

I wonder how long a man can live without a brain.

How old are you Dad?

together

1 Put in the missing letters.

(crossword)
- t ...
- o ...
- t _ g _ t _ _ r
- e
- t _ _ e _ h _ _ _
- h
- e
- r

2 Check the spelling of these words in your dictionary.

a climate — — — — — — — w......th...r

b wings are made of these — — f......t...ers

c to collect — — — — — — — g...the...

d another name for hide — — l......th...r

e a sister and a- — — — — — br...t...er

f a father and a- — — — — — m...th...r

3 Sort out these sentences. They must all begin with a capital letter and end with a full stop.

(a) to together go we church

....

(b) play garden we in the together

....

(c) together walk school to they

....

(d) cake a together bake will we

....

(e) see them often we together walking out

....

(f) homework their together boys the doing are

....

4 Find **together**. How many? [ ]

t	t	o	g	e	t	h	e	r	t	o
o	e	o	t	h	e	o	r	e	o	t
g	t	o	g	e	t	h	e	r	g	o
e	e	g	o	e	e	o	r	t	e	g
t	t	o	g	e	t	h	e	r	t	e
h	t	o	g	e	t	h	e	r	h	t
e	o	r	o	g	o	e	e	o	e	h
r	e	e	t	g	o	o	t	r	r	e
t	o	g	e	t	h	e	r	e	r	r

5 Collect words which begin with **to**.
Use your dictionary to help you.
Write on the back of this sheet if necessary.

....

....

If you had 20p and you asked your Gran for another 20p and your Grandad for 30p. How much would you have altogether?

20p

You don't know your Maths, boy.

You don't know my Grandparents!

Name _____   Date _____

 ,  ,  ,

following	where	place	different	without	together

Proof Reading

Read the story carefully. Some of the words are not spelt correctly. The words in the top box will help you. Underline the mistake and then write it as it should have been written.

morning, second, together, where, asked, found, walked, following, suddenly, places, number, first, inside, under, turn, often, round, coming, without, began, different, through, round, walked, started

My friend Sam came rownd this morrning. "Shall we play hide and seek insiyde?" he askt. We ofen play togethur at all sorts of differunt games.

"Yes, let's!" I said and starrted to think of plases wer I could hide.

"My tern to hide," Sam said, as he walkt threw the door.

I counted to the numbur 100, then shouted "I'm cuming!"

Withowt losing a secund, I beegan to look for Sam. At furst I was folowing Sam's dirty footprints but sudenlee they ended. I walkt all rownd the house. I fownd him, asleep undur my bed!

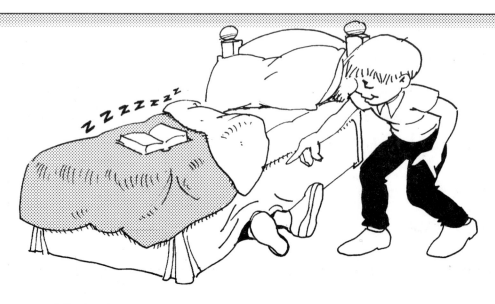

Proof Reading

Read the story carefully. Some of the words are not spelt correctly. The words in the top box will help you. Underline the mistakes and then write it as it should have been written.

> **brought, gone, right, number, knew, half, told, while, place, round, ask, opened, thinks, might, inside, asked alright, thought, write, stopped, watch, during, without, suddenly, morning**

27 High Street,
Bridgetown,
Yorkshire
YO7 4AB
14. 9. 98

Dear Emma,

Thank-you for the present which the postman brawt this morrning. He took it to numbur 25 but Sam, next door, new it hadn't gon to the rite plas. He came rownd and towld me what had happened. I opend the parcel and looked insiyd - what a lovely wotch!

My last one sudenley stopt working so I have been withowt one for a wile.

I askt my Mum today if you mite be able to stay with us durring the half term holiday. She said she thort it would be alrite. She will rite to your Mum and asc her what she thincs. So I miyt see you soon.

Love,

Jenny

Name .... Date ....

Proof Reading

Read the story carefully. Some of the words are not spelt correctly. The words in the top box will help you. Underline the mistakes and then write it as it should have been written.

during, brother, different, anywhere around, watch, always, does, places, second, between, think, show, together, goes, gone, morning, don't, brought, without, sometimes, never, often, anything, found, didn't

Durring the holidays Mum and I allways go on a shopping trip toogethur withowt my brothur and Dad. My brother dus not like shopping and nevur gose with us. Sumtimes we have dinner out, at diffrent plases. We have nevur gon back enywhere for a secund time. In the morrning we allways look arrownd the shops for a new outfit. Beetween us we donnt ofen go home withowt having fownd one! In the afternoon we go to the theatre to woch a show. Returning home, Dad allways says, "What have you brote me?"

I reply, "We didunt thinc you wanted enything!"